D0291977

On the Other Hand...

Jewish Words of Wisdom

On the Other Hand...

Jewish Words of Wisdom

Edited by Matt Silverman

BARNES
& NOBLE
BOOKS

NEW YORK

The quotes in this book have been drawn from many sources, and are assumed to be accurate as quoted in their previously published forms. Although every effort has been made to verify the quotes and sources, the publisher cannot guarantee their perfect accuracy.

ISBN 0-7607-5357-1

Printed and bound in the United States of America

04 05 06 07 08 HC 9 8 7 6 5 4 3 2 1

In memory of my mother and father,
whose wisdom I miss every day.

And for their help in preparing this book,
I thank the whole mishpocheh.

BENJAMIN DISRAELI, THE PRIME MINISTER OF GREAT
Britain (1868, 1874-1880) said, "The wisdom
of the wise, and the experience of ages, may be
preserved by quotation." That is the essence of
the book in your hands: to offer a portion of the
wisdom of the ages through quotations by, and
about, Jews.

You will find (and enjoy!) quotes from
authors of all religious backgrounds about Jews,
Judaism and that elusive quality "Jewishness."
Featured, of course, are quotes on these topics
and many others by Jews, some observant, others
skeptical, a few apostate.

The quotes were gathered from a variety
of sources: sacred texts, novels, poems, advice
columns, even songs and comedy routines.
Some of the quotes—and authors—are bitter,

poignant, occasionally tragic; others are light-hearted, irreverent and fun. Some are familiar, others nearly forgotten.

Proverbs and folk sayings, most derived from Yiddish, are sprinkled among the quotes from individual sources. In many of these traditional words of wisdom, there is the inevitable loss of richness and rhyme in the translation. I urge you to look for them elsewhere in the original languages. These quotations are unattributed, as are those in the chapter of Jewish curses. Otherwise, throughout the book, authors of the quotations are identified, and their dates of birth and death, along with a biographical word or two, are provided once.

The Talmud teaches that "When a man meets his Maker, he will have to account for those pleasures of life he failed to experience." I hope you will not fail to take great pleasure in your experience with the Jewish Words of Wisdom that follow.

–*Matt Silverman*

The Chosen People

For thou art a holy people unto the Lord thy God: the Lord thy God hath chosen thee to be a special people unto himself, above all people that are upon the face of the earth. The Lord did not set his love upon you, nor choose you, because ye were more in number than any people; for ye were the fewest of all people. But because the Lord loved you, and because he would keep the oath which he had sworn unto your fathers, hath the Lord brought you out with a mighty hand, and redeemed you out of the house of bondmen, from the hand of Pharaoh king of Egypt.

DEUTERONOMY 7: 6–8

Let me tell you something that we Israelis have against Moses. He took us forty years through the desert in order to bring us to the one spot in the Middle East that has no oil.

—GOLDA MEIR (1898-1978), Israeli Prime Minister

The Jewish people have been in exile for 2,000 years; they have lived in hundreds of countries, spoken hundreds of languages and still they kept their old language, Hebrew. They kept their Aramaic, later their Yiddish; they kept their books; they kept their faith.

—ISAAC BASHEVIS SINGER (1904-1991), writer

God, I know we are your chosen people, but couldn't you choose somebody else for a change?

—SHOLOM ALEICHEM (1859-1916), writer

The Hebrews have done more to civilize men than any other nation. If I were an atheist, and believed blind eternal fate, I should still believe that fate had ordained the Jews to be the most essential instrument for civilizing the nations.

—JOHN ADAMS (1735-1826),
second President of the United States

Being a Jew is like walking in the wind or swimming; you are touched at all points and conscious everywhere.

—LIONEL TRILLING (1905-1975), critic

If you prick us, do we not bleed? if you tickle us, do we not laugh? if you poison us, do we not die? and if you wrong us, shall we not revenge?

—SHYLOCK in *The Merchant of Venice* by
William Shakespeare (1564-1616), playwright

There is no greater compliment to the Jews than the fact that the degree of their unpopularity is always the scientific measure of the cruelty and silliness of the regime under which they live.

—SINCLAIR LEWIS (1885-1951), novelist

When I pray, I speak to God. When I study, God speaks to me.

—LOUIS FINKELSTEIN (1895-1991), President of the Jewish Theological Seminary

Nobody is stronger, nobody is weaker than someone who came back. There is nothing you can do to such a person because whatever you could do is less than what has already been done to him. We have already paid the price.

—ELIE WIESEL (1928-), author and survivor of Auschwitz and Buchenwald

If you ever forget you're a Jew, a Gentile will remind you.

—BERNARD MALAMUD (1914-1986), novelist

If my theory of relativity is proven successful, Germany will claim me as a German and France will declare that I am a citizen of the world. Should my theory prove untrue, France will say that I am a German, and Germany will declare that I am a Jew.

—ALBERT EINSTEIN (1879-1955),
physicist and humanist

(The Jews) have enjoyed rather too much history and too little geography.

—ISAIAH BERLIN (1909-1997),
philosopher and historian

To be a Jew is a destiny.

—VICKI BAUM (1888-1960),
novelist and screenwriter

Jewish Mothers (and Fathers)

The most remarkable thing about my mother is that for thirty years she served the family nothing but leftovers. The original meal has never been found.

—CALVIN TRILLIN (1935–),
author, humorist and fresser

A mother understands what a child does not say.

Always be nice to your children because they are the ones who will choose your rest home.

—PHYLLIS DILLER (1917–), comedian

Even a secret agent can't lie to a Jewish Mother.

—PETER MALKIN (1929–), Israeli intelligence legend

My mother loved children—she would have given anything if I had been one.

—GROUCHO MARX (1890–1977), comedian

My mother buried three husbands, and two of them were just napping.

—RITA RUDNER (1955–), comic

I didn't know he was a genius. Frankly, I didn't know what the hell he was.

—LEAH ADLER (1921–), mother of
Hollywood prodigy Steven Spielberg

Marriage is not just spiritual communion, it is also remembering to take out the trash.

—DR. JOYCE BROTHERS (1928–),
television psychologist

The father loves his son, and the son loves his sons.

—THE TALMUD

What my mother believed about cooking is that if you worked hard and prospered, someone else would do it for you.

—NORA EPHRON (1941–), writer-director

Toughness doesn't have to come in a pinstriped suit.

—DIANNE FEINSTEIN (1933–), U.S. Senator

Fathers and mothers have lost the idea that the highest aspiration they might have for their children is for them to be wise...specialized competence and success are all that they can imagine.

—ALLAN BLOOM (1930–1992), educator

A successful marriage is an edifice that must be rebuilt every day.

—ANDRÉ MAUROIS (1885–1967), author

The reason grandparents and grandchildren get along so well is that they have a common enemy.

—SAM LEVENSON (1911–1980), humorist

America

So, at last I was going to America! Really, really going, at last! The boundaries burst. The arch of heaven soared. A million suns shone out of every star. The winds rushed into outer space, roaring in my ears, "America! America!"

—MARY ANTIN (1881-1949),
author of *The Promised Land*, 1912

The twentieth-century ideals of America have been the ideals of the Jew for more than twenty centuries.

—LOUIS D. BRANDEIS (1856-1941),
U.S. Supreme Court justice

Even if you are Catholic, if you live in New York you're Jewish. If you live in Butte, Montana, you are going to be goyish even if you are Jewish.

—LENNY BRUCE (1925-1966), comic

My father never lived to see his dream come true of an all-Yiddish-speaking Canada.

—DAVID STEINBERG (1942-), comedian

Came Yom Kippur—holy fast day world wide
  over to the Jew,
And Hank Greenberg to his teaching and the old
  tradition true
Spent the day among his people and he didn't
  come to play.
Said Murphy to Mulrooney, "We shall lose the
  game today!
We shall miss him on the infield and shall miss
  him at the bat
But he's true to his religion—and I honor him for
  that!"

—"Came Yom Kippur, A Hank Greenberg Poem" by
  EDGAR GUEST (1881-1959). Greenberg was the
Detroit Tigers' Hall-of-Fame slugger who declined to
play in a 1934 World Series game on Yom Kippur.

I sent the club a wire stating:
PLEASE ACCEPT MY RESIGNATION. I DON'T
WANT TO BELONG TO ANY CLUB THAT WILL
ACCEPT ME AS A MEMBER.

—GROUCHO MARX

In the United States there is more space where nobody is than where anybody is. This is what makes America what it is.

—GERTRUDE STEIN (1874-1946), author

People are broad-minded. They'll accept the fact that a person can be an alcoholic, a dope fiend, a wife beater and even a newspaperman, but if a man doesn't drive, there's something wrong with him.

—ART BUCHWALD (1925-), journalist

Most Texans think Hanukkah is some sort of duck call.

—RICHARD LEWIS (1947-), comedian

In April 1917 the illusion of isolation was destroyed, America came to the end of innocence, and of the exuberant freedom of bachelor independence. That the responsibilities of world power have not made us happier is no surprise. To help ourselves manage them, we have replaced the illusion of isolation with a new illusion of omnipotence.

—BARBARA TUCHMAN (1912-1989), historian

God and Man

Everyone ought to worship God according to his own inclinations, and not to be constrained by force.

—FLAVIUS JOSEPHUS (C. 37–100),
Jewish-Roman historian and soldier

If God lived on earth, people would break his windows.

My religion consists of a humble admiration of the illimitable superior spirit who reveals himself in the slight details we are able to perceive with our frail and feeble mind.

—ALBERT EINSTEIN

Doubt is part of all religion. All the religious thinkers were doubters.

—ISAAC BASHEVIS SINGER

The world is new to us every morning—this is God's gift; and every man should believe he is reborn each day.

—BAAL SHEM TOV (C. 1698-1760), a.k.a. RABBI ISRAEL BEN ELIEZER, the founder of modern Hasidism

To you I'm an atheist; to God, I'm the Loyal Opposition.

—WOODY ALLEN (1935–),
writer, actor, director and kvetch

I rarely speak about God. To God, yes. I protest against Him. I shout at Him. But to open a discourse about the qualities of God, about the problems that God imposes, theodicy, no. And yet He is there, in silence, in filigree.

—ELIE WIESEL

Never let your sense of morals get in the way of doing what's right.

—ISAAC ASIMOV (1920–1992), writer

I once wanted to become an atheist but I gave up...they have no holidays.

—HENNY YOUNGMAN (1906–1998),
king of the one-liners

God will pardon me. It's His business.

—HEINRICH HEINE (1797–1856), poet and critic

God seems to have left the receiver off the hook, and time is running out.

—ARTHUR KOESTLER (1905–1983), novelist

If God, as some now say, is dead, He no doubt died of trying to find an equitable solution to the Arab-Jewish problem.

—I. F. STONE (1907–1989), journalist

Tradition

I was raised in the Jewish tradition, taught never to marry a Gentile woman, shave on Saturday and, most especially, never to shave a Gentile woman on Saturday.

—Woody Allen

Promises are the uniquely human way of ordering the future, making it predictable and reliable to the extent that this is humanly possible.

—Hannah Arendt (1906–1975), historian and philosopher

It is change, continuing change, inevitable change, that is the dominant factor in society today. No sensible decision can be made any longer without taking into account not only the world as it is, but the world as it will be…

—Isaac Asimov

The conventional is uncritically enjoyed, and the truly new is criticized with aversion.

—Walter Benjamin (1892-1940),
essayist and critic

The trouble with us is that the ghetto of the Middle Ages and the children of the twentieth century have to live under one roof.

—Anzia Yezierska (c. 1885-1970), writer

The tradition of all the dead generations weighs like a nightmare on the brain of the living.

—KARL MARX (1818-1883),
economist and philosopher

Men can know more than their ancestors did if they start with a knowledge of what their ancestors had already learned… That is why a society can be progressive only if it conserves its traditions.

—WALTER LIPPMANN (1889-1974), journalist

Everybody ought to have a Lower East Side in their life.

—IRVING BERLIN (1888-1989), composer

The pursuit of knowledge for its own sake, an almost fanatical love of justice, and the desire for personal independence—these are the features of Jewish tradition that make me thank my stars that I belong to it.

—ALBERT EINSTEIN

We seem to be going through a period of nostalgia, and everyone seems to think yesterday was better than today. I don't think it was, and I would advise you not to wait ten years before admitting today was great. If you're hung up on nostalgia, pretend today is yesterday and just go out and have one hell of a time.

—ART BUCHWALD

*Bei Mir Bist Du Schoen**: Love

When love is strong, a man and a woman can make their bed on a sword's blade. When love grows weak, a bed of 60 cubits is not large enough.

—THE TALMUD

To a wedding, walk; to a divorce, run.

* Sholom Secunda (1894–1974), songwriter-composer

A human being must love someone, otherwise he or she goes out like a candle.

—Isaac Bashevis Singer

Oh what lies lurk in kisses!

—Heinrich Heine

It isn't enough for your heart to break because everybody's heart is broken now.

—Allen Ginsberg (1926-1997), poet

A wise man, looking for a bride, should take an ignoramus along to advise him.

The magic of first love is our ignorance that it can ever end.

—BENJAMIN DISRAELI (1804–1881),
British Prime Minister

The heart is half a prophet.

In Biblical times, a man could have as many wives as he could afford. Just like today.

—ABIGAIL VAN BUREN (1918–),
author of the *Dear Abby* advice column

Love does not make the world go round, looking for it does.

—HERB GARDNER (1934–2003), playwright

Let's face it: if you're romantically involved, you're financially involved.

—Sylvia Porter (1913-1991),
financial advice columnist

Let's face it, everyone is the one person on earth you shouldn't get involved with.

—Nora Ephron

Dance at every wedding and you'll cry at every funeral.

He who is without a wife dwells without blessing, life, joy, help, good and peace.

—The Talmud

My wife Mary and I have been married for forty-seven years and not once have we had an argument serious enough to consider divorce; murder, yes, but divorce, never.

—JACK BENNY (1894-1974), comedian

Politics, Schmolitics

Sometimes we must interfere. When human lives are endangered, when human dignity is in jeopardy, national borders and sensitivities become irrelevant. Whenever men or women are persecuted because of their race, religion, or political views, that place must—at that moment—become the center of the universe.

—ELIE WIESEL

Those who won our independence by revolution were not cowards. They did not fear political change. They did not exalt order at the cost of liberty.

—LOUIS D. BRANDEIS

The most radical revolutionary will become a conservative the day after the revolution.

—HANNAH ARENDT

What a country calls its vital economic interests are not the things which enable its citizens to live, but the things which enable it to make war. Petrol is much more likely than wheat to be a cause of international conflict.

—SIMONE WEIL (1909-1943), philosopher

The only difference between the Democrats and the Republicans is that the Democrats allow the poor to be corrupt, too.

—OSCAR LEVANT (1926–1973),
musician and curmudgeon

Liberty is liberty, not equality or fairness or justice or human happiness or a quiet conscience.

—ISAIAH BERLIN

Surely half the population is more than a special interest group.

—BETTY FRIEDAN (1921–), feminist

Every major horror of history was committed in the name of an altruistic motive. Has any act of selfishness ever equaled the carnage perpetrated by disciples of altruism?

—AYN RAND (1905-1982), writer

When I bore people at a party, they think it is their fault.

—HENRY KISSINGER (1923-),
scholar and U.S. Secretary of State

Freedom of expression is the matrix, the indispensable condition, of nearly every other form of freedom.

—BENJAMIN CARDOZO (1870-1938),
U.S. Supreme Court justice

The first duty of a revolutionary is to get away with it.

—ABBIE HOFFMAN (1936-1989), revolutionary

America has given to the world a precious jewel. It has shown that a government whose concerns are purely secular and which leaves to the individual conscience of its citizenry all obligations that relate to God is the one which is actually the most friendly to religion. It is a precious jewel that we have. We should guard it well.

—LEO PFEFFER (1910-1993), jurist

There is no free lunch.

—MILTON FRIEDMAN (1912-), economist

I head a nation of a million presidents.

—CHAIM WEITZMANN (1874-1952),
Israel's first President

Politicians like to tell people what they want to hear—and what they want to hear is what won't happen.

—PAUL A. SAMUELSON (1915-), economist

The time is at hand when the wearing of a prayer shawl and skullcap will not bar a man from the White House, unless, of course, the man is Jewish.

—WALLACE MARKFIELD (1926-2002), novelist

Such A Smart Kid!

Teach thy tongue to say *I do not know* and thou shalt progress.

—MOSES BEN MAIMON, a.k.a. MAIMONIDES
(1135–1204), theologian

Many complain of their looks, but none complain of their brains.

Experience becomes possible because of language.

—NOAM CHOMSKY (1928–), scholar and activist

As a general rule the most successful man in life is the man who has the best information.

—BENJAMIN DISRAELI

History teaches us that men and nations behave wisely once they have exhausted all other alternatives.

—ABBA EBAN (1915–2002), Israeli diplomat

Some scholars are like donkeys: they merely carry a lot of books.

Science without religion is lame, religion without science is blind.

—ALBERT EINSTEIN

For a successful technology, reality must take precedence over public relations, for Nature cannot be fooled.

—RICHARD FEYNMAN (1918-1988), Nobel-laureate physicist who discovered the cause of the 1986 explosion of the space shuttle *Challenger*

The human brain starts working the moment you are born and never stops until you stand up to speak in public.

—GEORGE JESSEL (1898-1981), entertainer

Experiences are savings which a miser puts aside. Wisdom is an inheritance which a wastrel cannot exhaust.

—KARL KRAUS (1874-1936), writer

It is not the answer that enlightens, but the question.

—EUGENE IONESCO (1909-1994), dramatist

There are worse crimes than burning books. One of them is not reading them.

—JOSEPH BRODSKY (1940-1996), poet

The luck of the fool is this: he doesn't know that he doesn't know.

By the time you're eighty years old you've learned everything. You only have to remember it.

—GEORGE BURNS (1896-1996), entertainer

A bookstore is one of the only pieces of evidence we have that people are still thinking.

—JERRY SEINFELD (1954-), comedian

A wise man hears one word and understands two.

Understanding is a wellspring of life unto him that hath it; but the instruction of fools is folly.

—PROVERBS 16:22

You don't need a weatherman to know which way the wind blows.

—BOB DYLAN (1941–), singer-songwriter

L'Chayim (To Life)!

No matter how bad things get you got to go on living, even if it kills you.

—SHOLOM ALEICHEM

If you can't go over, you must go under.

Tragedy is when I cut my finger. Comedy is when you walk into an open sewer and die.

—MEL BROOKS (1926–), entertainer

Advice is what we ask for when we already know the answer but wish we didn't.

—ERICA JONG (1942–), author

A man should go on living–if only to satisfy his curiosity.

The real voyage of discovery consists not in seeking new landscapes, but in having new eyes.

—MARCEL PROUST (1871–1922), novelist

Don't worry about tomorrow, who knows what will befall you today?

Live well. It is the greatest revenge.

—THE TALMUD

I went on a diet, swore off drinking and heavy eating, and in fourteen days I had lost exactly two weeks.

—JOE E. LEWIS (1902–1971), comedian

The aims of life are the best defense against death.

—PRIMO LEVI (1919–1987), writer

I know that there are people who do not love their fellow man, and I hate people like that!

—TOM LEHRER (1928–), singer-songwriter

I am a butterfly drunk with life. I don't know where to soar, but I won't allow life to clip my beautiful wings.

—JANUSZ KORCZAK (1878–1942),
children's writer and educator

Experience is what you get when you don't get what you wanted.

—ANN LANDERS (1918-2002), advice columnist

Life is a dream for the wise, a game for the fool, a comedy for the rich, a tragedy for the poor.

—SHOLOM ALEICHEM

Razors pain you;
Rivers are damp;
Acids stain you;
And drugs cause cramp.
Guns aren't lawful;
Nooses give;
Gas smells awful;
You might as well live.

—DOROTHY PARKER (1893-1967), wit

The opposite of love is not hate, it's indifference. The opposite of art is not ugliness, it's indifference. The opposite of faith is not heresy, it's indifference. And the opposite of life is not death, it's indifference.

—Elie Wiesel

From your lips to God's ears...

Good And Evil

Conscience: that quiet voice which whispers that someone is watching.

—JULIAN TUWIM (1894-1953), poet

With or without religion, you would have good people doing good things and evil people doing evil things. But for good people to do evil things, that takes religion.

—STEVEN WEINBERG (1933-), author and physicist

If it turns out that there is a God, I don't think that he's evil. The worst that you can say about him is that basically he's an underachiever.

—WOODY ALLEN

God does not seek to destroy the evil nations, but their evil.

—SHOLEM ASCH (1880-1957),
novelist and playwright

The right to do something does not mean that doing it is right.

—WILLIAM SAFIRE (1929-), columnist

If you keep on saying things are going to be bad, you have a good chance of being a prophet.

—ISAAC BASHEVIS SINGER

Beware of those who talk about sacrifice.

—MURIEL RUKEYSER (1913–1980), poet

Let us be grateful to people who make us happy:
They are the charming gardeners who make our
souls blossom.

—MARCEL PROUST

The jungle is dark but full of diamonds…

—ARTHUR MILLER (1915–), playwright

The purpose of freedom is to create it for others.

—BERNARD MALAMUD

If you're going to do something wrong, at least enjoy it.

—LEO ROSTEN (1908-1997),
writer and Yiddish lexicographer

My guiding principle is this: Guilt is never to be doubted.

—FRANZ KAFKA (1883-1924), author

It's really a wonder that I haven't dropped all my ideals because they seem so absurd and impossible to carry out. Yet, I keep them, because in spite of everything I still believe that people are really good at heart. I simply can't build up my hopes on a foundation consisting of confusion, misery, and death. I see the world gradually being turned into a wilderness, I hear the ever-approaching thunder, which will destroy us too, I can feel the sufferings of millions and yet, if I look up into the heavens, I think that it will all come right, that this cruelty too will end, and that peace and tranquility will return again.

—ANNE FRANK (1929–45),
diarist who perished at Auschwitz

You Should Live
So Long

*Make sure to send a lazy man for the angel
of death.*

Old age is the most unexpected of things that can
happen to a man.
—Leon Trotsky (1879-1940),
Communist revolutionary and Soviet politician

Being an old maid is like death by drowning, a really delightful sensation after you cease to struggle.

—EDNA FERBER (1887-1968), writer

Your health comes first; you can always hang yourself later.

No one's death comes to pass without making some impression, and those close to the deceased inherit part of the liberated soul and become richer in their humaneness.

—HERMANN BROCH (1886-1951), novelist

He who is obsessed by death is made guilty by it.

—ELIAS CANETTI (1905-1994), writer

Don't ask the doctor, ask the patient.

Wisdom doesn't automatically come with old age. Nothing does—except wrinkles. It's true, some wines improve with age. But only if the grapes were good in the first place.

—ABIGAIL VAN BUREN

A man's worst enemies can't wish on him what he can think up himself.

Anyone who goes to a psychiatrist ought to have his head examined.

—SAMUEL GOLDWYN (1882-1974), movie mogul

To me, old age is always fifteen years older than I am.

—BERNARD BARUCH (1870-1965), financier and
Presidential advisor

*Never trust the man who tells you all his troubles
but keeps from you all his joys.*

Age to me means nothing. I can't get old; I'm working. I was old when I was twenty-one and out of work. As long as you're working, you stay young. When I'm in front of an audience, all that love and vitality sweeps over me and I forget my age.

—GEORGE BURNS

The Evil Eye: Jewish Curses

May all your teeth fall out except one, and that one should ache you.

May he win a lottery and spend it all on doctors.

May you grow so rich that your widow's second husband never has to worry about making a living.

May she grow two more hands to scratch all her itches.

May he back into a pitchfork and grab a hot stove for support.

May you have lots of money, but be the only one in the family with it.

May he marry the daughter of the Angel of Death.

May she have stones and not children.

May all the problems I have in my heart go to his head.

May she live in a house with a hundred rooms, and may each room have its own bed, and may she wander every night from room to room, and from bed to bed with a fever, unable to sleep.

May he get so sick as to cough up his mother's milk.

May leeches drink them dry.

May you laugh with lizards.

May she go crazy and run through the streets.

May they free a madman and lock him up.

May she grow a wooden tongue.

May God visit upon them the best of the Ten Plagues.

May a young child be named after him.

May I outlive him long enough to bury him.

May she see everything, but have no money to buy it.

As many years as you've walked on your feet, may you walk on your hands, and for the rest of the time you should crawl along on your ass.

May ten ships of gold be hers and the money should only make her sick.

May he have a large store, and whatever people ask for he shouldn't have, and what he does have, no one should ask for.

On summer days, may she mourn, and on winter nights, she should torture herself.

May he be a chandelier, to hang by day and to burn by night.

May their luck be as bright as a new moon.

May she have Pharaoh's plagues sprinkled with Job's scabies.

May you hang yourself with a sugar rope and have a sweet death.

May her stomach rumble so badly, she'll think it was a Purim noisemaker.

May you always wish for good luck.

May you grow like an onion, with your head in the ground and your feet in the air.

Mishpocheh: Family

I cannot think of any need in childhood as strong as the need for a father's protection.

—SIGMUND FREUD (1856–1939), psychoanalyst

I'd rather have roses on my table than diamonds on my neck.

—EMMA GOLDMAN (1869–1940), anarchist

A table is not blessed if it has fed no scholars.

Ask your child what he wants for dinner only if he's buying.

—FRAN LEBOWITZ (1950-), writer

Crazy geese, crazy goslings.

I have often been downcast, but never in despair; I regard our hiding as a dangerous adventure, romantic and interesting at the same time. In my diary I treat all the privations as amusing. I have made up my mind now to lead a different life from other girls and, later on, different from ordinary housewives. My start has been so very full of interest, and that is the sole reason why I have to laugh at the humorous side of the most dangerous moments.

—ANNE FRANK

There is no such thing as "fun for the whole family."

—JERRY SEINFELD

Never look in your sister's borsht.

—LAWRENCE SILVERMAN (1922-2003), historian

Seizing legislative and economic power is not the same as getting help with the dishes.

—NAOMI WOLF (1962-), author

Parents can give a dowry but not good luck.

My ambition is to be a good ancestor.

—HERBERT ZIPPER (1904-1997), music educator

"May you have joy from your children" was the greatest blessing conceivable. They were the parting words on happy and sad occasions. Honor brought to parents by their children was the accepted standard of measuring success.

—SAM LEVENSON

When a father helps a son, both smile; but when a son must help his father, both cry.

Work, or *Gelt* By Association*

Look at Jewish history. Unrelieved lamenting would be intolerable. So, for every ten Jews beating their breasts, God designated one to be crazy and amuse the breast-beaters. By the time I was five I knew I was that one.

—MEL BROOKS

* George S. Kaufman, (1889-1961), dramatist

Art is the symbol of the two noblest human efforts: to construct and to refrain from destruction.

—SIMONE WEIL

My first piece of advice is to "be lucky." That's not always easy, but one of the tricks is to recognize opportunity when it knocks.

—EDGAR M. BRONFMAN (1930–),
business leader and philanthropist

One man chops wood; the other does all the grunting.

Success and failure are both difficult to endure. Along with success come drugs, divorce, fornication, bullying, travel, medication, depression, neurosis and suicide. With failure comes failure.

—JOSEPH HELLER (1923–1999), novelist

I'd rather be a failure at something I love than a success at something I hate.

—GEORGE BURNS

You name it and I've done it. I'd like to say I did it my way. But that line, I'm afraid, belongs to someone else.

—SAMMY DAVIS, JR. (1925–1990), entertainer

Books and harlots have their quarrels in public.

—WALTER BENJAMIN

What marks the artist is his power to shape the material of the pain we all have.

—LIONEL TRILLING

I don't want to achieve immortality through my work. I want to achieve immortality through not dying.

—WOODY ALLEN

Learning is what most adults will do for a living in the 21st century.

S. J. PERELMAN (1904-1979), writer

Whatever it is in your power to do, do with all your might.

—ECCLESIASTES 9:10

Opportunities are usually disguised as hard work, so most people don't recognize them.

—ANN LANDERS

THE *EMMES:* TRUTH

A half-truth is a whole lie.

The absolute truth is the thing that makes people laugh.

—CARL REINER (1922-), comedian

Nothing is so difficult as not deceiving oneself.

—LUDWIG WITTGENSTEIN (1889-1951), philosopher

I cannot and will not cut my conscience to fit this year's fashions.

—LILLIAN HELLMAN (1905-1984), dramatist, to the House Un-American Affairs Committee, 1952

The free expression of the hopes and aspirations of a people is the greatest and only safety in a sane society.

—EMMA GOLDMAN

Emotions are not tools of cognition. What you feel tells you nothing about the facts; it merely tells you something about your estimate of the facts.

—AYN RAND

The eye is small—but it sees the world.

Ninety percent of the politicians give the other ten percent a bad reputation.

—HENRY KISSINGER

I never cease being dumbfounded by the unbelievable things people believe.

—LEO ROSTEN

The closer a man gets to knowing himself, the less likely he is to trip up on his own illusions.

—ARTHUR MILLER

What is lofty can be said in any language, and what is mean should be said in none.

—MAIMONIDES

In moral life, ignorance isn't all that common; dishonesty is far more so.

—MICHAEL WALZER (1936–), political philosopher

Be who you are and say what you feel, because those who mind don't matter and those who matter don't mind.

—THEODOR GEISEL (1904–1991),
author-illustrator of the Dr. Seuss books

If I Were a Rich Man...*

The rich swell up with pride, the poor from hunger.

—SHOLOM ALEICHEM

God will provide—ah, if only He would till He does!

* Lyrics from "Fiddler on the Roof" by Sheldon Harnick (1924-)

If you want to know what God thinks of money, just look at the people he gave it to.

—DOROTHY PARKER

Bankruptcy is a legal proceeding in which you put your money in your pants pocket and give your coat to your creditors.

—SAM GOLDWYN

It's no disgrace to be poor, but it's no honor either.

Everybody likes a kidder but nobody loans him money.

—ARTHUR MILLER

I have enough money to last me the rest of my life unless I buy something.

—JACKIE MASON (1934-), comic

Anything that has real and lasting value is always a gift from within.

—FRANZ KAFKA

If only God would give me some clear sign! Like making a large deposit in my name in a Swiss bank.

—WOODY ALLEN

Liberals feel unworthy of their possessions. Conservatives feel they deserve everything they've stolen.

—MORT SAHL (1927-), satirist

God loves the poor but helps the rich.

We who are liberal and progressive know that the poor are our equals in every sense except that of being equal to us.

—LIONEL TRILLING

Poverty was an ornament on a learned man like a red ribbon on a white horse.

—ANZIA YEZIERSKA

It's not that money makes everything good; it's that no money makes everything bad.

Money never remains just coins and pieces of paper. Money can be translated into the beauty of living, a support in misfortune, an education, or future security. It also can be translated into a source of bitterness.

—SYLVIA PORTER

Be A *Mensh*: Character

We who lived in concentration camps can remember the men who walked through the huts comforting others, giving away their last piece of bread. They may have been few in number, but they offer sufficient proof that everything can be taken from a man but one thing: the last of human freedoms—to choose one's attitude in any given set of circumstances—to choose one's own way.

—VICTOR FRANKL (1905-1997),
psychologist and Auschwitz survivor

Courage is a special kind of knowledge: the knowledge of how to fear what ought to be feared and how not to fear what ought not to be feared.

—David Ben-Gurion (1886-1973),
Israeli pioneer and Prime Minister

Judge a man not by the words of his mother, but from the comments of his neighbors.

—The Talmud

All excellent things are as difficult as they are rare.

—Baruch (Benedict) Spinoza (1632-1677),
philosopher

Pride is the mask of one's own faults.

Humility is no substitute for a good personality.

—Fran Lebowitz

Violence is the last refuge of the incompetent.

—Isaac Asimov

Above all things, never be afraid. The enemy who forces you to retreat is himself afraid of you at that very moment.

—André Maurois

When one must, one can.

The final test of a leader is that he leaves behind him in other men the conviction and will to carry on.

—Walter Lippmann

The best index to a person's character is (a) how he treats people who can't do him any good, and (b) how he treats people who can't fight back.

—Abigail Van Buren

A man is not honest simply because he never had a chance to steal.

My idea of an agreeable person is a person who agrees with me.

—Benjamin Disraeli

Perhaps too much of everything is as bad as too little.

—Edna Ferber

An angry man is unfit to pray.

—Rabbi Nahman of Bratslav (1772-1810),
Hasidic leader

You may be disappointed if you fail, but you are doomed if you don't try.

—Beverly Sills (1929-), opera singer

No man sins for someone else.

—The Talmud

If you have to choose character or intelligence—in a friend or in a candidate—choose character. Intelligence without character is dangerous, but character without intelligence only slows down a good result.

—GLORIA STEINEM (1934-), activist and author

If I am not for myself, who will be for me? And if I am only for myself, what am I?

—HILLEL (C. 60 B.C.E.-9 A.D.),
rabbi and interpreter of Biblical Law

It's so simple to be wise. Just think of something stupid to say and then don't say it.

—SAM LEVENSON